I0162307

Networking Personalities

How to Create Rapport and Build Confidence in your Business and Personal Relationships

Carol Merlo, M.Ed.

What People are Saying about Networking Personalities

Carol's book not only gives us important tools for effectively communicating with potential business partners and customers, but also for honoring our differences and bringing out the best in our team members. Every serious business person will want to know how to apply Networking Personalities.

Marian Head, Author, Revolutionary Agreements

If you are looking for a way to get on the fast track to business success, Networking Personalities is a must read. Applying the skills in this book will have a significant impact on every one of your business and personal relationships.

Terry Petrovick, Internet Marketing Entrepreneur

Not only did I gain insight as to how my own personality operates, I learned more about how to interact with AND support other Personalities.

Connie Godenick, M.D.

You may have attended workshops, listened to numerous audios, or read various books on this topic. Networking Personalities puts it all together in one place, with practical comparison charts, and insights to help anyone build a successful team.

David Rundle, Network Marketing Professional

Networking Personalities gives you insight into people's strengths and teaches you how to best connect with others. Often, the only reason we lack success is simply that we don't understand people, including ourselves!

Cheryl Townsley N.D.

Praise for the
Networking Personalities
Workshop

This was the single most effective training I have taken, since joining my company. I finally feel like I have some useful information that I can use in business and in my everyday life on how to talk to people the way they need to hear and learn, because it is not about me! I can apply this in my life every day.

Linda Sztanko

Thank you for researching and teaching us a vital aspect to not only being successful but to "love with power" through understanding Networking Types. You empowered me to transform my thinking to have confidence in my personality quadrant. I enjoyed how to discover what quadrant of personality I am to be more effective and to appreciate and love who I am instead of using that velvet hammer.

Satu Tanninen

This workshop opened my eyes to an understanding of individual personalities and how this can benefit one in every aspect of life, work, family, etc. I loved the hands on and the role-playing.

Helga Altmann

This workshop truly opened my eyes to see that different people respond to and react very differently from each other. I know now that I need to change my approach when speaking to various types of people. I loved the public introspection in a safe setting.

Juergen Harder

This was an excellent training for business and life. I have learned how important it is to be aware of others and how to respond to them in a way such that they feel important. Now I see how different personalities can work together as a team.

Jane Adamson

This workshop had great information and practical tools for improving my people skills that can be use with my business, my family, and my friends. I enjoyed the good information and slides. Carol is very demonstrative and upbeat.

Dr. Greg Roberts

The workshop was so helpful in helping me know how to relate to other Networking Personalities in building my business. I now see why some people may have been overwhelmed by my approach. I loved being able to see what my strengths and weaknesses are.

Lorinda Dyck

This is an excellent, interactive workshop. There were different ways of learning, self-awareness and development. Carol is a dynamic presenter. I loved the role-playing, the audience input, the handouts and the excellent presenter.

Rose Pric

ACKNOWLEGEMENTS

Special thanks to my mother Ann Beveridge, who originally encouraged my interest in psychology and introduced me to personality typing.

To my dear friends, Marion Head, Phil and Kathleen Peters, Bob Phillips, Christine Detrick, and Peggy H. MacKinnon Bendell for their attention to detail and valuable feedback in making this book more complete, understandable and impactful.

Finally, to my amazing husband Bill, who always cares enough to look deeply into my material, ask pertinent questions, and improve the quality of my work. Without his love and care, this book would not have been possible.

Table of Contents

The Three Keys to Successful Communication

- Understand your own Style, Gifts, and Challenges.

- Determine how People will Best Receive your Information.

- Match your Communication Style to their Receiving Style.

How to Create a
World Class Organization

If you are involved in any business that depends upon relationships for its success, you have come to the right place. Whether you are in the workplace or whether the workplace is at your home, your objective is to find people who want to improve their financial, interpersonal, and/or physical condition in life and to teach them how to achieve their goals through your vehicle. This is a wonderful objective and yet many people fail before they even begin because they do not understand the importance of creating optimum relationships with clients and co-workers and how easy it can be to modify our own communication styles to reach a broader range of people.

We are all uniquely different, but not so different from one another that we can't find and apply general principles about how to approach, teach, and motivate different styles of people. The key is to find either the greatest common denominator or greatest number of characteristics that are common among individuals or groups of people and then learn how to apply those commonalities to our communication efforts.

Historically, quadrant personality typing has been the easiest way to achieve an understanding of the differences and the commonalities between people. It has been used effectively to approach, motivate, and educate people throughout history.

I am sure you have been exposed to it in one form or another. People ascribe colors, animal names, or jewels to the styles to make their approaches seem to be unique. Nevertheless, the basic four styles are essentially the same in each of these methods.

My purpose in writing this book is for you to easily and simply identify various Networking Personalities of people and relate to them in a way that works for them so that you can improve the quality of your business and relationships. This is a simple process but it isn't always easy. Learning new behaviors takes an investment of time and energy but it is well worth it.

Are certain people 'better' at people skills than others are? Certainly! However, those people had to learn those skills somewhere in life in order to apply them to this business. No one is inherently gifted at communication. Some of us have had enriching early child experiences that encouraged successful communication but everyone has to learn and apply effective skills at some point in life. For the most people, it's a 'learn as you grow' phenomenon. If this is your goal, get ready to adapt and learn.

In order to sell something effectively, you need to understand why a person would buy what you have and then develop the skills that will enhance the probability of enabling that person to receive your information and make a buying decision.

Many of us make the mistake of basing our interpersonal communications on what interests us instead of taking the time to study behavioral cues that would increase the probability that what we are offering will be received. If we want to experience successful communication and persuasion, we must understand that our own interests are best served when we can convey the quality, consistency, and value of an idea or product in such a way that the person sees their WIIFM (what's in it for me).

This is important whether we are dealing with shorter-term relationships like those in business or at home, where the relationship you are creating with each person can be life-long.

It is also important to understand that whether we are dealing with sales, friendships, or even mates, we go through a filtering and selection process to make decisions, regardless of which style we have. Therefore, when we are sharing something with someone, we need to match our information and communication style to his or hers so they can more effectively receive it.

From that point, we can determine if the idea or product is a good fit for both that person and for ourselves. However, if we can't get behind the 'firewall' of their personality, that person won't be able to make an effective decision.

No matter which style you operate from, your personal growth is largely dependent of your willingness to focus on improving your communication skills by building on your innate strengths.

In this book, you will discover that each person, regardless of his or his style, is innately gifted with some skills and weak at others. Although you can improve your communication and relationship skills as you grow, be on the lookout for others who are naturally better where you are weak and team up with them.

Let's look at a basic business model and how people can work together to create an effective outcome to better illustrate the importance of creating a team.

First, a successful organization needs someone who is an effective recruiter/promoter to reach out to others and expose the product or service to them, unless you have an automated advertising campaign.

If you are not a strong recruiter/promoter, you will either need to develop these skills or hire someone to do it for you. Through trial and error, you can develop the skills to contact, engage, present to, and sell your product or service. If you are not willing to do this, even poorly — at first — you will not get very far. You need to have people buying your products in order to receive income.

Second, a successful business needs someone to do follow up and build relationships if you want to have retention. Some recruiters are great at 'getting them in' but they fail at 'keeping them in' because there was no relationship or caring established in the initial interaction. It's a rare product that produces loyalty without requiring a consistent, caring person to follow through with the end consumer. This becomes even more of a challenge in the social media age, where people can easily comparison shop, whether it's for a network marketing opportunity or a church community.

Third, a growing business needs someone who can educate others to do the above. Many sales people and managers can 'do it' but don't know how to 'duplicate' success. Therefore, we need to have someone who can create a system that everyone can follow and, once the system is in place, effectively train people to follow it. Systems allow a business to function effectively despite changes in personnel. When the manager is the 'center of the wheel' and there are no self sustaining systems, duplication of effort and extra hours are spent re-learning processes with new personnel.

Although many companies have trainers who can provide this service, every organization needs to develop some training and communication skills to get their people focused on a consistent and reliable system. Training goes beyond providing sales aids and manuals. It requires consistent follow up and accountability to ensure compliance with the system.

Fourth, any business needs people that can organize the office, respond to and organize emails, track the promotional materials, inventory, the marketing reports and pay the bills. This requires an entirely different set of skills from those of the promoter/recruiter because they aren't people skills but rather data skills.

Without a good organizer, an organization may fall apart because customers will fall through the cracks. I have found very few excellent, open, people-oriented individuals who can also stay organized, maintain good records and create or print reports. Therefore, they need to have an organizer on their team.

Finally, I believe we all need to hire, partner with, and become a mentor and accountability partner with others. Nothing builds an organization like a person who can see the best in others better than they can see it themselves. Author Napoleon Hill was instrumental in helping people understand the power of having a Mastermind Group composed of mentors and accountability partners. If you have not read Think and Grow Rich, I highly encourage you to do so.

No one will ever become a master of all of the above skills and we will always be better at some of the skills than others. As you apply the material in this book, you will begin to notice the natural inclinations and skills of the various styles that people use to communicate and function.

As you apply the material in this book, you will begin to notice the natural inclinations and skills of the various types of people that come into your organization and into your life. Once you become adept at recognizing and understanding Networking Personalities, you will learn to relate to people from their point of view. This will help them excel at their natural inclinations to develop those skills that they aren't versed in to create better relationships and a more fulfilling life. This book will teach you the elements you need to build those skills.

The Elements of a Great Team

You might be thinking, "if only I could be more open, friendly, influential, persuasive, and knowledgeable, I would be more successful than I am now". Well, there is more to the story...

Roger is one of those people that you might think you would want to have in your business. He is in the top 10% of sales closed in his company. He has won every incentive the company has offered and any time you talk to him, he is excited about the company and his future in it.

The problem? He is in a business that is dependent upon repeat sales to achieve a high level of income. Roger doesn't follow up, build relationships, or support others to share the opportunity and so does not experience the type of income that could be available to him.

Those of us who are not like Roger might think, "if only I could be like him...then I would be successful at this." The interesting thing is that Roger might be thinking, "If only I could be more organized and do more follow up, then I could be really great at this."

Many people overlook opportunities because they don't understand the importance of appreciating who they actually are. As a result, they don't develop their strengths or find those people who can complement their weaknesses with the skills to build a strong team and a successful organization.

The 'Who am I' Question

I can remember the first time I became aware of my Self. I was 11 years old and was standing under a basketball hoop on the playground at school. It was like coming out of a dream into the real world for the first time. As I looked up at the strings on the hoop, I realized that I was a self; unique and independent of any other self. I was 'Me'. This was a lonely - yet freeing experience.

That was when I came to realize that because I have independent thought, I could make my own decisions. I did not have to do what my parents or teachers said and could make decisions based on my beliefs and interests. (I later learned that the brain goes through various cognitive stages as it matures, and this was just a new stage in my development.)

This experience was so profound for me that over the next few years I read as much as I could about 'who am I' and personal development. This grew into a lifetime love of psychology. I was driven by the need to understand people and put their behavior into perspective. I wanted to make friends and be popular, so I read as much as I could to figure out how to do this. (Ironically, the more popular people were doing, rather than reading).

This is what I learned:

To be effective at personal development we need to understand the difference between the things we can change about our ourselves, (our characteristics or 'state') and the things we can't (our temperament or 'traits').

The dictionary www.dictionary.com defines personality as 'the aggregate of features and traits that form the individual nature of some person or thing'. We typically think of our personality as a combination of attitudes, beliefs, sense of humor, moods, speaking style, gestures, and mannerisms. Most of us sense that we are born with some inherent personality traits that are the result of our biological genetic coding, which determines how our personality expresses itself. These traits form our involuntary habits, determine our preferred way of gathering information and influence the choice of words we use to communicate with others, as well as how we learn.

Nevertheless, it is difficult to attribute genetic factors to personality and conclude that we are born with our personalities in place. In other words, personality is malleable. Current scientific research has so far shown that only child disinhibition (how inhibited or uninhibited you are) has been shown to be a significant predictor of adult personality characteristics.

What this means from a physiological standpoint, is that some people have a predisposition for higher levels of physiological arousal to environmental stimuli, which includes our responses when exposed to and interacting with people. Because of this, such people develop inhibitions, which make them more shy and uneasy in social situations. I like to call this quality "inherent sensitivity." This sensitivity may also become repressed in highly sensitive individuals, and that person may express aggressive insensitivity as a result.

In contrast to these inherent qualities, the learned components of personality are called characteristics. Our characteristics reflect the behavioral patterns we develop from the decisions we have made as a response to our life experiences. Our characteristics differentiate us from others, and establish how we express our identities to the outside world. Our characteristics are responsible for the formation of habits, comfort zones, quirks, and idiosyncratic behavioral patterns

Temperament + Characteristics = Personality Type

Think of your personality type as your automatic pilot. It creates the involuntary behavioral patterns necessary for you to function and survive. Your type is your own personal road map that guides you toward the outward direction you take in life. Its characteristics influence what you become. It affects your self-image, self-esteem, self-confidence, and self-worth. It motivates you, creates your irritations, and controls stress and how that stress affects you. It is not a self-fulfilling prophesy, however.

Personality influences the way you face life's challenges and how you cope with them. It is the organizing principle that affects your sense of reality and spirituality. It greatly influences your health and overall sense of well-being.

We can change our attitudes, thoughts, feelings, and behaviors if we follow the simple techniques covered in this book. It isn't always easy and requires a commitment to getting the outcome we desire. Because most people have formed their personalities by adulthood, re-forming them on a significant level is exceptionally challenging, but with work, we can adapt to match the characteristics of others when communicating and relating.

*****

You can Control your Characteristics. States, in Contrast to Traits, are Changeable.

*****

Motivational trainers and psychotherapists all know that we have the ability to change habits, thoughts, and behaviors through intention and practice, but because we have certain inborn traits and impulses, some things will never change about us. Efforts to do so have resulted in emotional pain, mental illness, self-loathing, and even suicide because people decide that they aren't 'good enough' the way they are.

One of the biggest errors people make in personality typing is that they assume that they are a certain style because they believe who they actually are is somehow wrong or inadequate, so they should be something else.

People usually attempt to change their God-given traits because they did not receive adequate attention, affection, or approval from the people who were important to them when they were children.

In fact, many people don't ever actualize their true selves because of the influences of parents, institutions, or other factors that suppress them in an effort to control them and make them fit in to a particular social model.

The recognition of and development into becoming who we actually are, in contrast to who we are currently being, is a process that most people address as they grow into leadership roles. Personal development programs help fill this important need of teaching people how to develop leadership skills.

So, as you read this, remember that people can change much of whom they are being in the world but certain behavioral styles and talents will remain fixed throughout their lifetime. It is our job to accept and love that in ourselves and in others if we want to experience any level of comfort in life.

What I Can Change About Myself (character):

_____

_____

_____

What I Can't Change About Myself (Temperament):

_____

_____

_____

Discover Your
Networking Personality

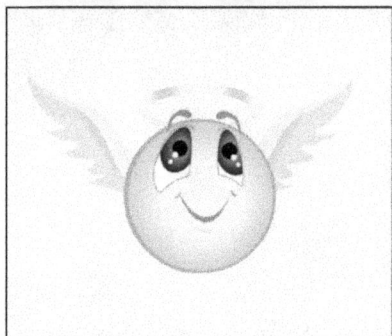

Quadrant personality typing typically assesses where a person is on two dimensions, and then places that person's style into a box. The next section will introduce you to the various dimensions that determine these styles. You can also take the free online personality test at www.CarolMerlo.com to help you determine your style.

We will use the following dimensions to determine your style:

- Whether you are people or task oriented
- Whether you are outward or inward focused in your thinking and behavior
- Your primary career orientation
- Which basic outcome drives your behavior

There Is No Right or Wrong Place to Be. Your goal is to be able to determine these characteristics in others so that you can more easily create rapport and communication.

Imagine you are in a room full of people who all want to learn about their personality style. First, let's divide everyone into one of two groups — the people who are people-oriented and the people who are task-oriented. This is the first dimension upon which we determine styles.

People	Task
Friendly, Warm	Reserved, Formal
Likes to touch when talking	Keeps a personal space
Easily shares feelings	Keeps feelings private
Relaxed about time	Disciplined about time
Spontaneous	Prefers to plan
Uses feeling words	Uses thinking words

Pauline is married to a dynamic businessperson named Terry. Each of them contributes value to their business in a complementary way. Terry is a person who immediately puts people at ease when they are around him. People feel comfortable communicating with him.

Although Pauline cares deeply for people, her passion is in accomplishing tasks. People don't always feel immediately comfortable around her. She feels great when everything comes out on time, when the bases are covered and when everything is 'done'. Pauline is Task-Oriented.

Task-Oriented people like everything spelled out and clear. Conversely, People-Oriented people are more tolerant of ambiguity. People-Oriented people like to have options and don't want to be constrained by time, commitment, or definition. Task-Oriented people like to have targets, mean what they say, and say what they mean, which includes being on time and valuing sequence.

Task-Oriented people want the job done, so will sacrifice the feelings of others if it means they can accomplish the goal. These people have a strong ability to categorize, itemize, plan, and execute tasks and objectives, and sometimes see people as being in the way of the accomplishment of a task.

People-Oriented people, however, are more interested in the relationships they create. They are interested in the outcome, of course, but they have a much more refined sense of what another person is feeling, and typically will create alliances to get their goals accomplished. They tend to be more relaxed and easy-going, will take time to converse and laugh, even if it means that the job may not be done on time.

Where are you on the People/Task Continuum?

Next, let's divide the people in the room by a different characteristic; whether they are more Outward or Inward focused.

Outward	Inward
Talks first	Waits to be approached
Decisive	Slower to decide
Looks outward for solutions and opportunities	Looks inward to avoid possible pitfalls
Expressive	Sensitive
Impatient	Patient
Opinionated	Reserved
Makes it happen	Experiences it happen

Outward people become impatient more easily than Inward people do and have a need to take action quickly. Inward people don't like to be rushed. They are looking for pitfalls in taking any forward action, so need time to make sure everything will turn out okay. Depending on their People/Task orientation, they will either be more concerned about the person or about accuracy than making quick decisions.

The degree to which you are Outward or Inward was largely hard-wired into you. Although you can modify your behavior to adapt, your tendency when too hungry, angry, lonely, or tired (under stress) will be to move toward your natural inclination. In a business that demands reaching out to others, many Inward people believe that they can't do it. (But they can, as you will see). Inward people are usually more sensitive to the behaviors of others and can get overwhelmed easily, so can readily take on this false belief.

Where are you on the Outward/Inward Continuum?

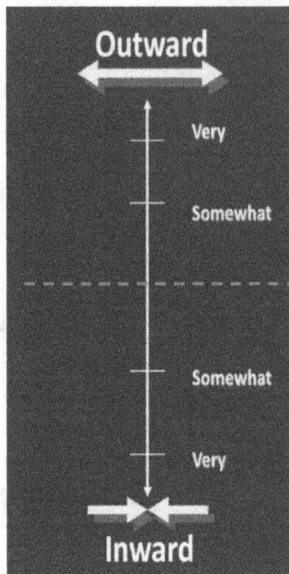

It requires a lot of energy for an Inward person to be outgoing. Introverted people have higher levels of physiological arousal, so they are easily conditioned by environmental stimuli. Because of this, they develop more inhibitions, which make them more shy and uneasy in social situations.

Inward people like to know the precise steps, scripts, and processes in order to recruit people. Because it is not natural for them to be assertive, they need a structure to depend on. If they are provided with a script and structure, they can learn to duplicate success and become good Leaders.

Where are you on this continuum? When entering a room full of people, do you feel happy and energized or uncomfortable and shy? Are you soft spoken or are you boisterous? Are you on the extreme end of the continuum or closer to the middle?

Place Yourself in this Grid

Let's look at the combination of the four characteristics.

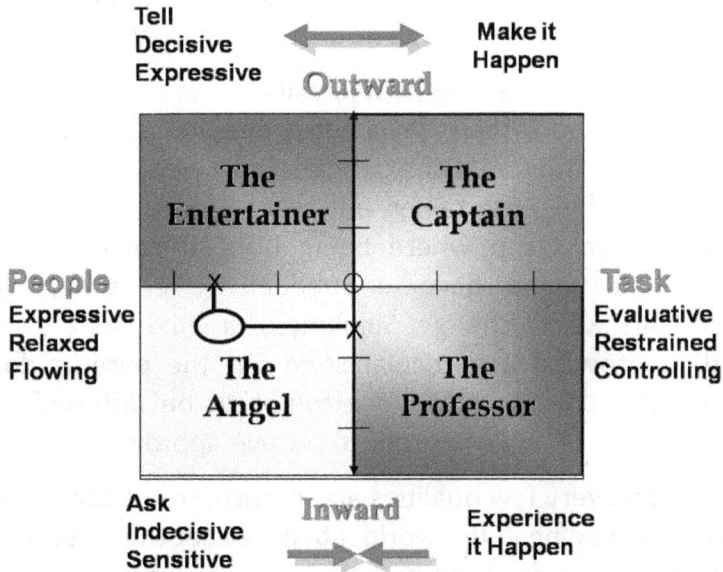

If you are Outward and People-Oriented you are an Entertainer. If you are Outward and Task-Oriented, you are a Captain. If you are Inward and People-Oriented, you are an Angel. If you are Inward and Task-Oriented, you are a Professor.

Unsure of your Style?

Don't worry if you can't completely fit yourself into a specific box. We are all unique and no two of us has the same combination of these characteristics.

There are infinite combinations of Personality styles. Imagine that the four squares below are overlaid by a grid, which contains billions of points. Each of us is somewhere on this grid. You might end up in the middle of two styles, on the far extreme of a style, or very close to the center.

As you can see from the graphic below, as we get closer to the middle, the styles merge into shades of gray.

You may also notice that people will change their behaviors depending upon their level of freedom, security, and comfort in a situation. For example, if you were an outgoing, warm, and fun Entertainer but were forced to live in a concentration camp where being noticed could get you killed, you would become subdued. Over time, your personality would change. Similarly, if a child has a strong tendency toward a particular style but the parents don't value that style, a child will attempt to be different and modify his or his style in order to receive approval and love.

Remember, very few qualities are in-born, so we can change who we are being in the world. I believe that the freedom to be authentic comes from being in a supportive environment where an individual can express his gifts and experience successes, as a result.

Some of the people who attend my workshops believe they are one style when they are actually someone completely different at their core, particularly when they believe that their style will not provide the recognition, results, relationships, or rationale they are seeking. From the outside, it's relatively easy to tell if a person is people or task, outward or inward. From the inside, our judgments about who we are can prevent us from seeing ourselves as we actually are.

A Universe of Uniqueness:
The Sub Styles

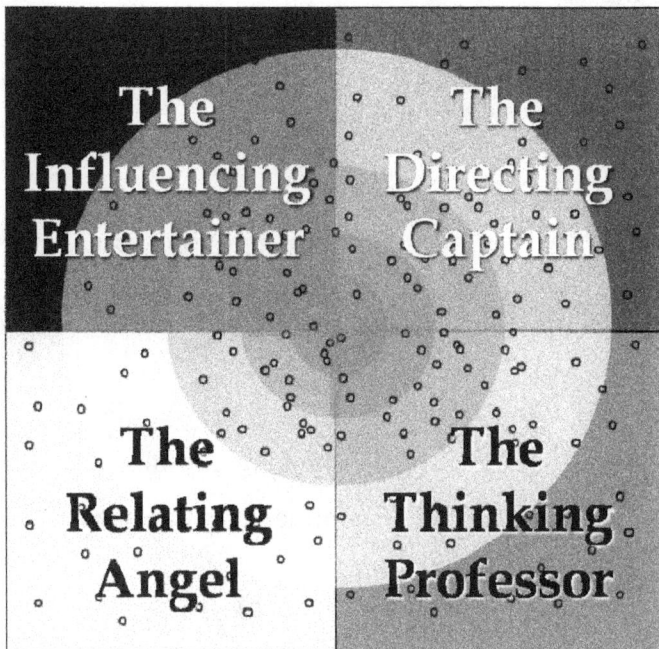

The Influencing Entertainer	**The Directing Captain**
The Relating Angel	**The Thinking Professor**

We typically fall into a major style and then a Sub style. Each of the four quadrants has four Sub styles. Depending on where you are in the grid, you will incorporate the characteristics of second Personality style and become a blend, taking on the characteristics of any of the four of them. You might think that the goal is to become the Center, but your particular flavor of Self is your unique expression and something-God Given, so be willing to get to know your true identity and embrace it.

Angels can be:

Relating Angels	Thinking Angels
Directing Angels	Influencing Angels

Entertainers can be:

Relating Entertainers	Thinking Entertainers
Directing Entertainers	Influencing Entertainers

Professors can be:

Relating Professors	Thinking Professors
Directing Entertainers	Influencing Entertainers

Captains can be:

Relating Captains	Thinking Captains
Directing Captains	Influencing Captains

My Secondary Style is

_____

If you are still unsure of where you fit on the grid:

Think about how you were as a child or what you are like when you are completely relaxed and feeling confident.

You may express different qualities at home than at your job. Think about areas in your life where you feel the most comfortable and notice who you are being in those situations.

Ask some of your closest friends how they see you. Remember, becoming who you actually are is a life-long process.

Pick the style that is least like yourself first.

How We Act Under Stress

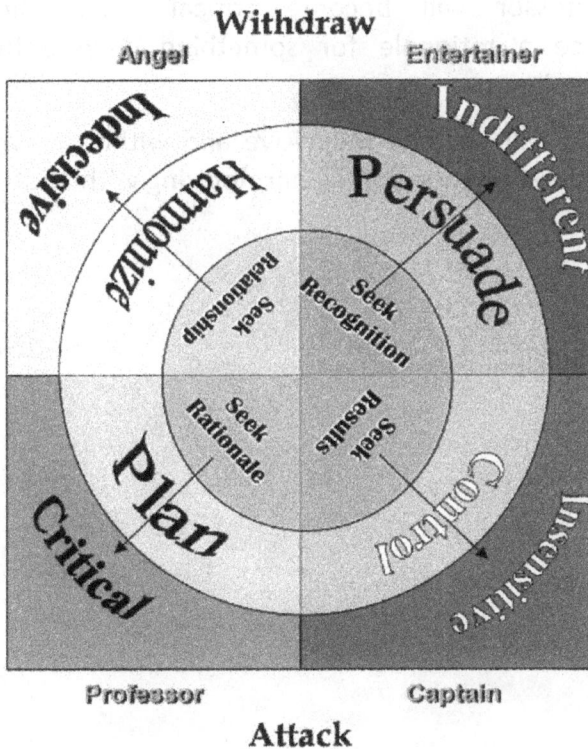

People-oriented people will typically withdraw from situations that involve conflict to preserve relationships, whereas task-oriented people will attack to force results, even if it requires being passive-aggressive. Task-oriented people experience greater pressure to achieve when under stress, so will push to get a job done and risk alienating people, whereas the people-oriented style will withdraw from people to find a solution and spare another's' feelings.

The Entertainer seeks recognition by using persuasion and sociability. When she is not recognized, she will withdraw and become indifferent and uncaring.

The Captain seeks results by controlling the environment. When she can't get the results she wants on time, she will reject and become insensitive and hurt peoples' feelings.

The Professor will become critical when she can't experience a rationale for something despite her best efforts to plan.

The Angel will become indecisive and withdraw when she can't create a relationship by harmonizing with another.

Test Your Knowledge

See if you can identify the type of personality each statement is connected to:

- Here's an idea. What do you think?

- I really enjoy working with you.

- Tell me how I can make a fortune at this quickly.

- Oh this is so much fun!

- I am so busy with my charity, church, and PTA. Plus, my family takes a lot of my time.

- What are the compliance rules?

- Did you hear that Sally has just joined?

- Here's how we are going to do it.

- How are you feeling?

- You handle it. Keep me informed.

- This event will blow you away!

- That presentation touched my heart.

- Give me all the facts on this.

Personality and The Art of War

I spent my childhood in libraries, in nature, and in the classroom where I felt comfortable in the world of theory. I loved doing science experiments and had a good sense of music, so learned the guitar and sang. In school, I would fall asleep while listening to history and political science. I didn't like battles and guns or memorizing their dates. To me, these topics were 'stupid'. I also didn't want to have anything to do with business or finance. After all, I was an artist!

Therefore, as many young adults, I was unprepared to take care of myself when I got out of school. I was inept when it came to doing banking or negotiating a job interview to earn a living and rise in the world of business. I didn't know how to use a checking account or even that I needed to put oil in my car regularly. It took most of my early adulthood to figure out that art must become a business if you want to eat, and businesses are run using the same skills as those used in politics, sports, and war.

In graduate school I started reading business management books and discovered that there is a common terminology regarding leadership styles among business theorists, team sports, and the military.

The terminology is similar because all business endeavors require the same types of leadership styles in the utilization of people and energy. War games predominate in business and sports. Therefore, if you want to succeed in business or in interpersonal relationships, it is important to understand the mechanisms of winning a battle, even if you are an artist like me!

Each of these methodologies is naturally correlated with one of the Networking Types:

The Entertainer is Tactical

The Captain is Logistical

The Angel is Diplomatic

The Professor is Strategic

As you read the following methodologies, think of how you typically lead your team. This will help you refine your identification of your style.

Strategy – The Why

A strategy is an overall plan, method, or series of maneuvers for obtaining a specific goal or result. The most effective battles are won when a good strategy has been formulated first.

Strategic thinking is extremely valuable in determining the direction in which your business goes in order to accomplish your 'Why'. Strategic Leadership involves the ability to anticipate, prepare, and position your team for the future.

Professors are the strategic system builders. They will create the systems but will not be the implementers of those systems, preferring to move on to another creative problem to solve.

Logistics – The How

Logistics takes the system the Professor created and focuses on the planning, implementation, and coordination, which includes the overall management of how resources are moved to the areas where they are required. Logistical Leadership is more interested in the 'How', or implementation method of the strategy. Logistics is vital to the success of any project. With logistics you can have the right people in the right places at the right times to accomplish the best results.

A logistical leader can easily determine the timing needed in all areas from getting tools to distributers and setting up conference calls, to knowing when to follow up. He or she will be able to devise training sequences and ensure materiel and information will be in the right place at the right time. The flow of function in space and time is the fascination.

Do not assume logistics is a passive activity! Logistics drives our businesses to make them grow more efficiently and effectively. The Captain, as a logistical Leader, will utilize you the Strategist's map, give you the steps to follow, train you, and hold you accountable for meeting your goals, and then leave you to your own devices.

Don't expect a lot of sympathy, however. Logistics is all about task management and implementation of the system. If you want results, follow the logistical leader's directions.

Tactics – The When and Where

Tactics involves making moves to better one's position -- where the action currently is -- to achieve a goal. A good tactician will scan for opportunities, look for the best angle of approach, and come up with a plan of immediate action for the greatest advantage.

Tactics for Entertainers involves persuasion, promotion, artistry, and improvisation. They can turn on a dime and have fun at the same time. They are inspirational and full of ideas.

The strategy can have been created and communicated, the logistics can have been done to ensure the data and materials are where they need to be, but without a target and the tactic, the strategy can fail. A good tactical leader will come up with great ideas for the next move to make in order to create success. It's up to the logistical leader, however, to help you determine which tactic is best for the desired outcome.

Diplomacy – The Who

Remember Roger who was a salesperson but didn't have repeat business? Well, Roger needs a few diplomats on his team. Any endeavor can go awry if the relationships between the members of the team aren't built and maximized or even if communications with the leader of the 'opposing team' fail. The diplomat is the relationship builder and peacemaker.

The Angel, as a diplomatic leader, enhances team loyalty and commitment, which is essential to the survival of any organization in today's competitive, global economy.

Diplomatic leaders have the innate ability to put personal feelings aside, avoid anger, and by doing so are highly successful in resolving conflicts. People love diplomats.

Follow up, relationship building, and people skills in general are the glue that holds an organization together. Angels, as natural diplomats, are typically the ones to build a long-term business with loyal associates.

Which is your most natural orientation? Typically, each person is uniquely gifted in one of the four, which corresponds to their Personality style.

Circle Your Most Natural Leadership Interest

Strategy   Tactics   Logistics   Diplomacy

How to Create Rapid Rapport

Once you become good at identifying Personality styles you need to begin the process of creating rapport. The science of NLP (Neuro Linguistic Programming) can show you how matching the physical mannerisms of another can create rapport. Rapport is the foundation for any meaningful interaction between people.

When you are in rapport with another person, you have the opportunity to create a sense of trust and emotional availability that would not be there if you do not have complementary Personality styles.

Have you noticed that when people enjoy being with each other, they have a tendency to use the same words or phrases, or dress in a similar way or have matching body language? For example, observe a group of teenagers who are friends and notice the similarities in their clothing, their choice of words and how they walk or sit.

Conversely, people who are not in rapport have different postures, gestures, voice tonality or don't make eye contact. This illustrates the concept - the more we are like the other person (or the more we have in common), the more we like the other person.

There is a great deal of scientific substantiation for this phenomenon. Researchers at the Boston University Medical School studied films of people having conversations. The researchers noticed that the people talking began to unconsciously co-ordinate their movements (including finger movements, eye blinks and head nods.) When they were monitored using electroencephalographs, it was found that some of their brain waves were spiking at the same moment too. As the conversations progressed, these people got into rapport.

How to Match and Mirror

Matching and mirroring is a powerful way of getting an appreciation of how the other person is seeing/experiencing the world. The key element within establishing and maintaining rapport is your ability to pay attention to the behavior of the other person, the ability to match it, and then adapt as you see their responses. You have to be able to see what they are doing with their body and then you copy it.

It is also important to match the person's verbiage, accent, and vocabulary. You should notice whether a person is using words that correspond to a particular sense: visual, auditory, or kinesthetic. Work on using the same words as the other person. Pay attention to the micro-behaviors of those we wish to influence.

Any observable behavior can be mirrored, for example:

Hand and Arm Gestures

Spinal Alignment

Inflection and Vocal Variety

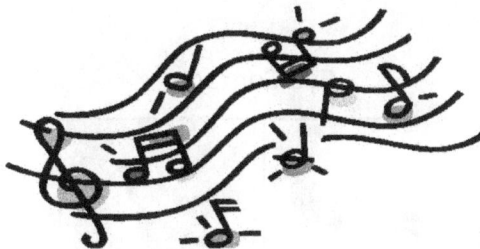

For voice, you can match tonality, speed, volume, rhythm and clarity of speech. All of us can vary various aspects of our voice and we have a range in which we feel comfortable. If someone speaks very fast, much faster than you do and at a rate at which you would not feel comfortable; match this person by speaking faster, while staying within a range that is comfortable for you.

Rate of Speech

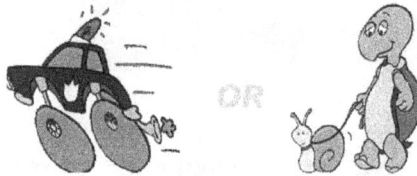

Body Posture

Eye Contact

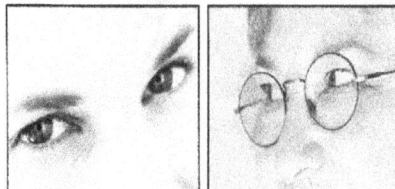

Social Space

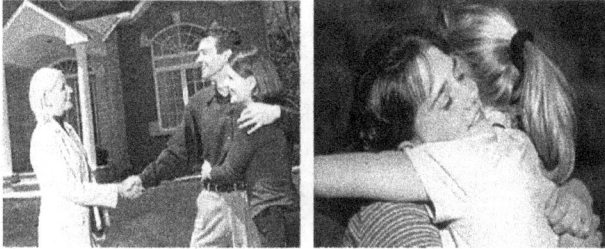

Mirroring Exercises

If you want to experience a quick increase in your communication skills, you must practice intentionally. Many times I will learn something from a book or a class and think how great it would be to integrate it into my behavior but then the day goes by and I forget to try it out!

So, now I make sure to leave the house with the specific intention of practicing a particular skill. Be sure to take the time to practice these exercises so that you will eventually develop competence in creating rapport.

Exercise 1

- Find someone to have a conversation with. Do not tell the person initially that you are going to be mirroring him or her during the conversation.
- Start the conversation by asking for his or her opinions about various subjects.
- As you are listening, start to mirror the other person's physiology, including voice tone and tempo.
- Notice how the person is sitting or standing and match it by slowly moving your body to copy theirs.
- Before ending your conversation, let your partner in on what you were doing, make sure you have reestablished rapport by once again physically mirroring your partner.

Exercise 2

- Practice mirroring people on television (chat shows & interviews are ideal.) You may be surprised at how quickly you can become comfortable as you subtly mirror the behaviors of others.

Exercise 3

- Choose a safe situation to practice mirroring one element of someone else's behavior. When you have mirrored them for a while and think you are in rapport with the person, scratch your nose. If they lift their hand to their face within the next minute or so, congratulate yourself - you have led their behavior! Skilled communicators have a wide range of behaviors they can mirror to build rapport. You can find a way to mirror virtually anything you can observe.

- The fact that you've read this far means that you can see the benefits of increasing your rapport skills. Reading is sadly not enough - practice is the key to building skill, so do the exercises. When you first start the practice of mirroring, you may have to pay some conscious attention to what you're doing. After a while, however, you will start to catch yourself doing it unconsciously. This is where you really begin to build rapport elegantly!

Practice

Start practicing with the people in your immediate environment. You may wish to start with family members and begin to match different aspects of their posture, gestures, voice and words. Have fun with it and see if they notice what you are doing. At work or socially, start by matching one specific behavior and once you are comfortable doing that, and then match another. For friends with whom you really feel comfortable, notice how often you naturally match their postures, gestures tone of voice or words. Matching comes naturally, what you need to do is learn how to do it with everyone, then matching will become automatic whenever you wish to deepen your rapport with someone.

How to Apply this Information

On the next several pages, you will learn to become an expert at identifying and dealing with each of them and I have provided a handy 'cheat sheet' at the end, which you can tear out and take with you to help you determine Personality styles.

Let me tell you why developing this one skill is so important to your success in life. In order to succeed in any business, you will need to understand that you can develop effective communication and relationship skills regardless of your style, but it will take continuous effort and connection to your 'Why'.

You will need to re-read and study this book and apply these skills until it becomes second nature to recognize the different Personality styles and adjust your approach to relate to them.

Is it worth it? Let me tell you what this information did for me…

Once I figured out that I was a Thinking Captain, I had to come to terms with the liabilities involved in that and see the value in being a who I am, as well. I had had the mistaken idea that only Entertainers were any good at all in the business of persuasion so everyone should be like them.

Because I wasn't as good at people skills as I was at task skills at the time, I naturally wanted to improve in my weak areas. This wasn't easy but it was necessary to accomplish my goal of being an effective leader in my business and to help others become successful.

I did lots of personal development work to become better at my people skills and made a lot of mistakes along the way. I was determined to succeed so was willing to pick myself up and try again each time I didn't perform to my standards, hurt someone's feelings or lost a friend. I also learned how to pick my people. It can be easy to believe that you should be able to create rapport with everyone and maintain all friendships. At the end of the day, what matters is aligning with those people who make you feel good about being yourself. Working with others to accomplish a goal, however, requires work, and as you improve, your sense of social competence will improve.

What I had been missing until recently was that when I can determine someone else's Personality style, I can adapt my approach, meet their needs more effectively, and be more successful because I am more effective at communicating and dealing with people in a style that relates to their personality. It wasn't so much about changing my style as relating to other styles comfortably by changing my approach to meet their needs.

I now have the confidence that I know how to interact with others. When I am working with Angels I know that I need to slow down and spend a few minutes chatting with them about their life, being interested in their feelings, and asking open-ended questions before I get down to the bottom line. Because I am a Captain, and crave results, the result I am looking for is a good working relationship, so will take the time to do this.

When I am dealing with Professors or Angels, I can expect to have more than one conversation to get them engaged in what I am interested in.. I focus on relaxing and not be concerned if they aren't interested the first time because I understand their need for follow up and consistency. When I am dealing with Entertainers, I can speed up, get excited, and be ready to have fun. I can focus on them and make them feel important by listening, laughing, and enjoying their stories without being concerned about the accuracy of their details. Moreover, I don't have to be upset when they are late. Instead, I can anticipate that and either be a little late myself text them ahead of time and come prepared with something to fill my time while I am waiting.

I can quickly provide Captains with what they need to make a decision to move business forward. I can provide information they can use to create results and make quick decisions. I can provide them with what they need to help me so we can both get results that are more effective in our businesses. I don't anticipate that I will feel liked or affirmed.

Which people on your team are innately gifted in skills that you can to help develop so that they can make a better contribution to your entire team? Who else do you need on your team in order to fill the gaps so you can have a dynamic organization?

Who are the great promoters on your team? If you are good at follow up, help them by creating relationships with their people. If you are great at promotion, find someone who is good at relationships and have them team up. If you are great with people and your office is a mess, get an organizer to help you. Find those people whose strengths will complement your weaknesses.

Become an observer of behavior and be on the lookout for those types of people you could add to your team to help it become more balanced and successful.

Become Adaptable

How Angels Can Adapt

- Say no
- Take some risks
- Delegate
- Share their honest feelings with safe others
- Stop worrying about how it will affect others.

How to Adapt to Angels

- Support their feelings by showing personal interest
- Assume their take things personally
- Give them time to develop trust in you
- Slow down and be informal with them
- Show that you are actively listening
- Show them that what you are proposing is safe.

How Entertainers Can Adapt

- Control their time and emotions
- Become more objective (Time, Place, Form, Event)
- Keep their word
- Concentrate on the job at hand
- Focus on double-checking and organizing.
- Slow down
-

How to Adapt to Entertainers

- Support their opinions, ideas, and dreams
- Be upbeat, stimulating and fast paced
- Allow for digressions and long discussions
- Don't argue

- Spare them the details
- Show them that what you are proposing can enhance their image and visibility.

How Professors Can Adapt

- Show concern and appreciation for others
- Initiate new projects
- Use policies as guidelines, not laws
- Collaborate by seeking common ground
- Try short cuts and time savers on occasion
- Make timely decisions

How to Adapt to Professors

- Support their thoughtful and well-prepared approach.
- Show commitment through your actions
- Be detailed, accurate, and logical.
- Don't exaggerate.
- List the advantages and disadvantages by providing solid evidence.
- Assure them your proposal won't cause loss.

How Captains Can Adapt

- Relax and pace themselves
- Practice patient, open listening
- Develop sensitivity and empathy
- Notice they value of others and tell them about it.
- Slow down and become more cautious
- Identify with the group

How to Adapt to Captains

- Support their goals and objectives
- Reduce the small talk and get to the point
- Use facts, not feelings to disagree.
- Be well organized and precise
- Support your perspective with brief, logical analyses.
- Be firm but friendly.

Networking Personalities in Detail

What follows is a general description of each Personality style — how they act, how they sound, what drives them, and how to sell to them. Now, you may see yourself in one of the styles but don't feel you quite fit. That is normal. Remember the billions of points in the quadrants? No two human beings are exactly alike, so we are looking for tendencies, rather than absolutes here.

What Drives Each Personality Type?

Each style has a unique need that they are trying to fill. Our job is to recognize that need and help them fill it. When you can help a person feel great about who they are, you are more likely to maintain that relationship and build a strong, enduring business. In fact, people will express negative, critical, or self-destructive behaviors when they don't have the opportunity to fulfill their basic drive.

Entertainers crave Recognition

Captains crave Results

Angels crave Relationship

Professors crave Rationale

One of the biggest mistakes people make is to provide someone with the wrong answer to a need. Clearly, asking questions is fundamental to determining a person's Personality style and providing a solution to the underlying emotional need of an individual.

You will create loyalty in your group and empower more people to become leaders when you fulfill what that individual wants and

Who's Who in Social Media?

The ways in which we communicate today have gone beyond simply face to face or voice to voice. Today we communicate via texts, tweets, and posts. We rarely consider who are readers are and how we are coming across. Typically we use fewer words and only convey information by using pictures and videos to tell our stories.

In order to develop a following as a leader, it helps to understand how to reach the greatest number of personality types with your written communications. This includes email and websites.

Let's look at some emails and evaluate which type sent it. Hint-- Look for People vs. Task and Outward vs. Inward.

- I just want to let everyone know that I spoke with Fred right after our call and he was in utter shock and disbelief when I told him about the issue!

- I felt so sorry for Joe on the call...we do NOT need him to be having a heart attack over his job...he is truly one of the best assets we have. It's not only a shock to us but to him, as well.

- Steve felt SO sorry for us and will do everything he can to fix it for us.

- We WILL overcome this one too, my friends!

- We obviously still have some problems. The people in x department need to be taught to ask the question, "how will this affect the people in the y department?", before they go off and do something. Then, run it by someone who knows.

- Don't they know anything about Negotiating? You have to "give something but you never put everything on the table at once.

- You can "clean the toilet" without sticking your hand all the way down the drain.

- Pass this on, we all need to know how bad this really is.

- Most of you know what a fanatic I am about not passing on information about just about anything until checking to see if it is a hoax and/or urban legend.

- However I found the following in a mainstream online news source which virtually NEVER reports on alternative medicine or anything else that isn't totally mainline and provable.

- So imagine my delight to NOT find this information listed as fraudulent on my favorite exposé sites, such as snopes.com, hoaxbusters.org and urbanlegends.com (i.e. double negative means it is likely true) and to find the information contained to be validated by further research which I have listed below the main article.

- Joe, Scientific American July issue is great. Get a copy. "Hijacked Cells - How tumors Exploit the Body's Defenses." Sally

Entertainers

People-Oriented
Outward
Recognition Driven
Tactical Leaders

I ran into Melody at a party recently. Her Personality style is easy to spot. He shows up late because she "had a lot to do" before she came and got a little lost on the way. She walks into the room with a queenly air and just knows the party wasn't complete until her arrival. She is dressed in bright colors; you can hear her loud guffaws from across the room, even with the music playing and the sounds of other partygoers close by.

She walks up to the first person she sees and introduces herself with a flourish. She immediately starts talking about herself in a friendly way and usually makes everyone laugh very quickly.

She talks a lot and most people may not get a word in edgewise unless they interrupt her. It usually takes her a bit longer to tell a story because it has lots of embellishments and personal anecdotes in it. She doesn't notice when people are losing interest.

Robbie comes in. He is an extreme Entertainer. Robbie hugs everyone he talks to in the room and says something funny. He always has a group of people around him and loves being the center of attention. He has lots of influence and is always #1. Everyone loves Robbie!

Entertainers never meet a stranger. They lend electricity to the environment and to the people around them. They live life at the level of a gourmet feast and they bring to work and play a sense that something delicious is about to happen. Wherever they are, the atmosphere takes on a glow, seems brighter, more colorful and charged with an excitement that others often admire and even envy.

For an Entertainer, to be without impact or to make no difference in human affairs is what Tony Allesandra says is like being 'deprived of oxygen'. They hunger to make a splash, make something happen, to have a piece of the action, and to hit the big time.

Why You Need an Entertainer on Your Team

Entertainers are the best tacticians because they live in the present and see opportunities in events and people that strategists and logistical people may overlook.

How to Recognize an Entertainer

Tells Stories, Expressive, Dominates the Conversation

Word Usage

- Will include you in the conversation
- Tell stories and jokes
- Here's an idea...
- I feel this is the way to...
- Tell me what you think about...
- My sense is that...
- Switches from one topic to another easily
- Words are more about people than about things

Vocal

- Speaks fast
- Variety in inflection
- Vary pitch of their speech

Visual

- Facially animated
- Lots of hand gestures
- Spontaneous touching
- Big hand shakes
- Can't sit still

Key Qualities

- Impressed by recognition, excitement, and other outgoing people
- Love to have fun
- Like to avoid conflict
- Get bored easily
- Quick due to impatience
- Motivated by the ability to influence others
- Talk about themselves
- Not detail oriented
- Make decisions too quickly without much thought
- Optimistic
- Not good at follow through

What Drives an Entertainer?

Little Judy sashays into a room full of adults. She announces loudly that she can do cartwheels and wants everyone to watch her. 'Look at me, look at me', she says. Entertainers are driven by 'look at me', too. They want to be noticed and in the spotlight. It's difficult for an Entertainer to sit and listen. Like children, they 'just want to have fun'. If an activity doesn't appear to be fun relatively quickly, an Entertainer will get bored and either move to another activity or create a situation that causes 'fun' to happen, which might not be fun to everyone else.

Entertainers continuously seek approval and are motivated by accolades, especially if that approval is public.

Entertainers are at the center of influence in most business organizations. The opportunity to be in the spotlight, influence people, and have fun without time constraints or the confinement of the corporate setting makes the Network Marketing or Performance Arts industries an ideal business model for this style.

How Entertainers Operate in Business

- They just wing it and start talking to everyone enthusiastically and let others deal with the details.
- They have a good time with people and are at the center of attention at gatherings.
- In social situations, they are continuously making new friends even as they interrupt others to tell stories and show off.
- They can have huge parties that everyone attends because they all know how much fun it will be.
- Everyone will be talking about what a great person that Entertainer is!

How an Entertainer Talks:

There is enthusiasm in the Entertainer's language. Because they are people-oriented, they will use feeling words, rather than thinking words and they will usually connect one person to another, using their names.

The underlying message you get when listening to the Entertainer is, "So… where do we go from here? I know you are going to just love this!"

The Four Sub Styles of Entertainers

Influencing Entertainer

- Friendly and fun. Life of the party.
- Needs recognition to maintain energy
- Optimistic and happy
- Will start activities but not finish them
- Avoids detail and conflicts

Directing Entertainer

- Highly resourceful
- Persuasive
- Has a large network of contacts
- Can delegate and take charge
- Doesn't follow through

Relating Entertainer

- Charming
- Sees life as an exciting drama
- Empathetic and overly subjective
- Great at getting people together
- Gets bored easily

Thinking Entertainer

- Inspirational and enthusiastic
- Impulsive
- Fascinating conversationalist
- Can improvise easily
- Takes on too many projects

How to get an Entertainer's Buy-in

- Talk about how easy and fun it will be to do this.
- Emphasize how your product or service will provide recognition and excitement.
- Act upbeat and enthusiastic.
- Be brief and allow for flexibility.
- Tell stories instead of relating facts.
- Show the big picture, not the details.
- Ask an open-ended closing question like, "Where do we go from here?"

- They will respond well to 'everyone's doing it' or 'this offer will expire soon.'
- They might over-buy and have buyer's remorse, so be sure to help them make a decision that they won't regret later.

After the Commitment

- Send them the details of the transaction but be willing to handle the details for them and oversee their purchases.
- This style is most likely to regret a purchase or get bored, so remind them that they made the right choice.
- Show them innovative ways to use your product and be sure they are using the it correctly. They probably didn't read the directions.
- Have regular up beat social interactions with them in a relaxed setting.

Captains

Task-Oriented

Outward

Results Driven

Logistical Leaders

The organization brings a team of top Leaders together to help create a new program. Derrick has made sure he is part of this group because he knows that he has all the answers and without him, the whole system will fall apart.

He is not afraid to step on some toes to make sure the company runs right. He can hurt some feelings without paying too much attention and doesn't consider that much of a problem. He talks fast and rarely says something designed to nurture, encourage, or harmonize the group.

To Derrick, the group dynamic is not as important as the task. He is passionate about making it work well and fast. He has already worked out the logistics and knows the best route to take, so expects to lead the way.

Derrick believes that most of the people on the team are irrelevant because he already has all the answers, and unless he has done some personal development work, he will consider a team unnecessary because he has all the answers.

In fact, the majority of Derrick's ideas are sound and his uncanny sense of how to put methods and strategies together actually makes a better system for the company, despite his manner.

If you want a fast moving, goal-oriented and focused team, get a Captain. They are among the most competent and efficient people you can meet. They are so self-directed that if you were to follow up with them for more than a brief 'touch base' they would be offended and think you thought they were incompetent.

Captains want all the control for themselves because they believe they can get it done right and on time. They don't want to take the risk of delegating the process to someone who may not do it as well or as quickly because they are very clear about how to accomplish the job effectively. Unfortunately, they can hurt some feelings and bruise some egos in the process.

This doesn't mean that Captains don't have feelings. Some are highly sensitive to rejection and simply don't understand that their behavior puts people off. The great Captains improve their people skills to get great results.

Captains like to have their accomplishments recognized.

Why You Need a Captain on Your Team

Captains have the unique ability to see the goal and, at the same time, see what it takes in terms of skills, energy, and time needed to accomplish that goal. They make great Logistical Leaders.

How to Recognize a Captain

- Little Detail, Fast Paced, Gives Orders
- Word Usage
- Tell me what the goal is
- I don't want excuses
- Write this down
- Poor at small talk
- Won't state the obvious or repeat things
- Does not like to go from topic to topic without finishing one first
- Uses precise language

Vocal

- Intonation carries an implicit challenge
- People may feel they are being insulted by the Captain's tone of voice
- May sound impatient but not actually feel that way.

Visual

- Firm handshake
- Emphatic
- Movements are fast, suggesting impatience
- Steady eye contact

Key Qualities

- Avoids the irrelevant and the redundant
- Quick-focused
- Loves accuracy, precision, and clarity
- Believe they can overcome any obstacle
- Can juggle lots of tasks and responsibilities and do them all well
- Act as if they are the only ones with the answer
- Decisive
- Time conscious
- Highly territorial
- Controlling

What Drives a Captain?

Captains are propelled by an inner need to be in charge. Because they believe they know the best and fastest way to accomplish things, they are highly sensitive to allowing others to take over and ruin it. The fear that it may be done poorly, late, or not at all compels the Captain to be in charge at all times. Trust in the outcome and in people is the Captain's ongoing challenge.

How Captains Operate in Business

- They make a quick business plan, tell their manager exactly what they think without much sense of humility, and implement massive action strategies using a proven marketing mechanism.
- They hold their team members accountable to required team calls and track weekly progress reports.
- They review their team's work and hold them accountable.
- This gives them control, yet still frees them to line up bigger challenges.
- Their teams grow quickly and competently if the team members are secure in themselves!

How a Captain Talks:

When they talk to you, you will get the impression that the they are very busy and don't want to spend very much time talking to you. You may feel that you are not liked or are irrelevant. The Captain is so focused on the task that she assumes you are competent, so don't need much explanation or nurturing. Sentences are filled with orders, rather than requests, and there are no stories, explanations or adjectives. The underlying feeling is "Tell me yes or tell me no, but tell me quick 'cause I've gotta go."

The Four Sub Styles of Captains

Directing Captain

- Motivated by new opportunities
- Loves to give structure to organizations
- Likes to move on to new conquests
- Wants to have final say
- Takes charge of situations

Influencing Captain

- The most sociable of all the styles
- Concerned with relationships as well as wanting to get things done
- Needs to feel appreciated for what he/he gives to others
- Does not like being told what to do

Relating Captain

- Charismatic
- Likes results more than people
- Likes to plan ahead
- Will cut corners to reach goals efficiently
- Driven to achieve

Thinking Captain

- Highly responsible
- Organizes orderly procedures
- Wants it done right and gets impatient with incompetence
- Loyal
- Goals and standards are higher than in other styles

How to get a Captain's Buy-in

- Show up on time.
- Do not give directions or orders.
- Allow them to control the conversation.
- Provide all the pertinent information they need to make a decision on the first meeting.
- Get to the bottom line, the logic behind it, and the reasons to make a decision quickly without too many details.

- Talk about the results they will get from using your product or being involved in your opportunity.
- Give them specific options for buying and make sure you have the data to back up each option, and then ask a qualifying question, like, "Which registration pack do you want?"
- Ask a closing question that can be answered with a Yes or No. You can ask, "Do you want to purchase this product?"

After the Commitment
- Be sure to send them follow up information outlining your commitment to achieving results with them.
- Follow up often because they may go to a competitor.
- Ask if you delivered what you promised.
- Talk business. Do not ask what they would consider to be personal questions.

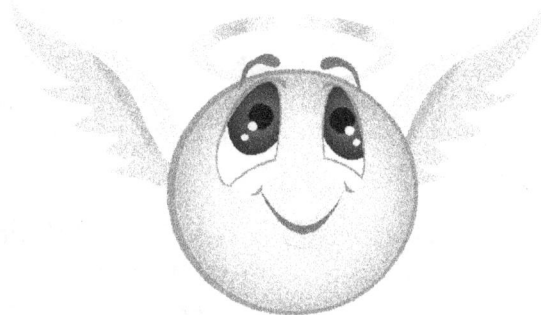

Angels

People-Oriented

Inward

Relationship Driven

Diplomatic Leaders

Glenda shows up at the party with a warm smile on her face. She looks around at the people in the room to find someone she knows. Walking up to someone, she immediately establishes eye contact with her friend and asks a question that is personal but not invasive and then listens intently.

Glenda, like most Angels will talk with one person at a time to establish a feeling-based connection with them. She would never consider getting loud and would rather be off, engaged in one-on-one conversations with people. Glenda loves to include others in her vision by using tact and friendship as a way to encourage them to join her. She has the unique ability to be able to see the best in people and create teams that can accomplish projects easily and work well together.

Glenda is highly sensitive to the emotions of others and can enable her team by taking care of them too much, so not develop independent leaders. She knows she needs to take care of her own needs by nurturing herself in order to be effective as a Leader.

Angels are soft spoken and casual. In conversation, they move from a few particulars to sweeping generalizations and jump from details to larger meanings. Because they are so people oriented, they will remember names easily and expect you to know the people whose names they mention. They usually remember details about a person's personal life and will take the time to ask about the family and other more personal subjects.

Enthusiasm, which makes them full of life and awareness, is what characterizes an Angel Leader. Their enthusiasm is based on something within themselves: an idea, mission, purpose, or passion. They want you to value, recognize and appreciate their 'true self.'

Because of their love of detail, you will notice that Angels will give you a blow-by-blow description any time they are telling a story. They want to be sure to tell you it was Wednesday, not Thursday, that they lost 4 pounds, not 5, or that it was in 1996 that Mary got her tonsils out.

Angels love lengthy, intimate conversations and feel that the more details they know about you, the better they can fill your needs and take care of you.

Angels are nurturers and will often give gifts as an expression of appreciation and friendship. To feel fulfilled, they need to feel that they are making a difference and helping others to give them a sense of accomplishment.

Why You Need an Angel on Your Team

Angels are natural Diplomats and have tremendous skill in managing negotiations, handling people, etc., so that there is little or no ill will as a result. When people work together in harmony, they are more likely to enjoy the process of winning the war and Angels 'keep them in the game'.

Angels will follow up, make sure everyone gets to the meeting, bring the tools and food, and make sure everyone has a good time. They will know when anyone is having problems and has all the details. They provide the glue that keeps the team together.

How to Recognize an Angel

One on One, Focused on Feelings, Supportive

Word Usage

- Starts sentences with, "I feel"
- How is 'specific family member'?

- Let me help you
- I hope you don't mind if I...
- How will this affect people on a day-to-day level?

Vocal

- Speaks slowly
- Soothing, even vocal tone
- Projects warmth and sincerity in their voice

Visual

- Balanced eye contact
- Hand shake is more tentative than strong

Key Qualities

- Empathetic
- Good listener
- Believes that goodness is everywhere in everything
- Trusts intuition more than the surroundings
- Loves stability
- Likes small groups of in-depth relationships
- Gets hurt feelings but won't tell you
- Doesn't rock the boat
- It's not whether you win or lose, it's how many friends you have that counts
- Seldom shows emotional peaks or valleys
- Doesn't like making big decisions
- Views actions as being louder than words
- Will avoid direct commands but will use illustrations and analogies to make a point

What Drives an Angel

Because Angels place people above tasks, they are driven to create harmony at all costs. Consequently, they see conflict as aversive and they will subordinate their own goals, interests, and activities to those of the people around them unless they work on assertiveness issues.

How Angels Operate in Business

- They listen to their Manager at length about what exactly they should do and how to align together as they grow the organization.
- They gather a loyal support team, and make sure they all have the materials they need.
- After drawing up or finding a step-by-step plan, they ask their people to work as a team, using the same system and tools.
- They see to it that everyone perseveres by encouraging them, having frequent one-on-one conversations and being a friend.
- Their projects are done earnestly, methodically, and thoroughly. Members of an Angel's team swear working with the Angel is the most fulfilling experience of their lives.

How an Angel Talks

Rather than using commands, like the Captain style, the Angel's language is filled with questions that are focused on the emotions of the person they are talking with. The Angel does not want to hurt, rush or demand an answer from people.

The Four Sub Styles of Angels

Relating Angel

- Easy to approach
- Cares deeply about a few special relationships or causes
- Does not like to attract attention. Works behind the scenes.
- Looks for ways to be of service
- Logic is optional

Directing Angel

- Driven and goal oriented
- Sets schedules and meets deadlines
- Makes sure things get done
- Enjoys being industrious
- Does not see the big picture

Influencing Angel

- Likes being with people but likes the focus on others
- Starts and sustains harmonious relationships
- Projects a warm, caring attitude
- Likes displays of affection and approval
- Does not plan or prepare

Thinking Angel

- Precise in thought and language
- Approaches new tasks cautiously
- Can detect contradictions easily
- Likes checklists
- Very detail oriented

How to get an Angel's Buy-in

- Break the ice with a brief personal comment.
- Ask about their family or service work.
- Mention the name of the person who referred you to them.
- Offer relationships as a benefit.
- Focus on wellness and wholeness.
- Emphasize the service you will provide.
- They may not ask for information because they are concerned about pleasing you more than getting their own needs met. Be sure to help them feel comfortable in getting all their questions answered.
- Tell them how your follow through will be designed for their personal situation.
- Show how much you care about them.
- Give them a guarantee.

After the Commitment

- Give them consistent, hands-on follow through.
- Provide them with a simple way to communicate with you about their progress, so they know you are involved in what they are doing.
- Show them specific steps to do the tasks they will need to undertake.
- Maintain a friendship by calling regularly and having quality time.

Professors

Task-Oriented

Inward

Rationale Driven

Strategic Leaders

Professors are often lower key and more soft spoken than any other style. They are typically efficient, curious, experimental, non-dogmatic, complex, impersonal, and independent. They try their best to be accurate and to sort things out.

Many Professors can be very articulate but may not be sensitive to signals that the listener has had enough and that they need to listen, too. They tend to talk past a listener's receptivity threshold.

Problem solving is a 24-hour occupation for a Professor. If they don't have a problem, they will find one to exercise their skills in developing models, maps, and paradigms. Although they aren't very 'touchy-feely', they deeply care. They experience being cared about by being asked to talk about their opinion and then listened to.

Because Professors are so focused on being exact and understanding precisely, you will see them correct others' language, ask questions to ensure clarity and attempt to eliminate any ambiguity in a conversation.

Although Professors are Inward, their sense of intuitively understanding the emotional cues given off by others is limited. Rather, they are particularly sensitive to the world of thoughts, ideas, and concepts.

Professors are critical, by nature. Because they are constantly evaluating data for accuracy, any inconsistency is painful, so they will point out errors and any incorrect information.

Why You Need a Professor on Your Team

Professors are excellent strategists because they love to analyze situations and data. You will increase the likelihood of achieving success in your enterprise by having a system to follow and Professors create systems. You need a good Professor on your team to evaluate the costs vs. benefits and set a course for everyone to follow, and to set an alternate course if one particular strategy isn't working.

How to Recognize a Professor

Detailed, Logical, Wordy

Word Usage

- Let's look at this logically
- What are the guidelines?
- Talks about data and features
- Will qualify statements with words like probably, usually, likely, etc.
- May use highly technical terms
- Will notice when others use words incorrectly and correct them
- Depending on the Sub Style, language is filled with possibilities, premises, hypotheses, and theorems
- Prefers theories and abstractions and likes to have data and facts to validate them

Vocal

- Uses the least inflection of any style
- They enunciate their words clearly
- Sounds neutral and objective

Visual

- Few facial expressions
- Not inclined toward touching

Key Qualities

- Dependable, detailed, factual
- Careful and cautious
- Sees the glass as half empty
- Desires order, accuracy, perfection
- Has trouble making decisions because they 'don't have all the facts', so procrastinates
- Prefers tasks over people
- Patient, cautious and thorough
- Wants clearly defined priorities and pace
- Willing to do the task alone
- Will share information only on a 'need to know' basis
- Hard to be persuaded otherwise once a decision is made. Loyal to their team and company

What Drives a Professor

Professors need to know and understand. They love to accumulate more and more useful knowledge, rarely deleting or forgetting any, and to work continuously on solutions to the many problems that intrigue them.

They want gratitude from others and want to be praised for being thorough. Professors like it when you ask them questions to show you how much they know.

How Professors Operate in Business

- They take the business very seriously, expecting to be judged by their attention to detail.
- Laboriously, they plan a great complicated, complete and accurate system, including all the science and compensation information.
- They figure out how each team member can build the business on his or his own, in case they can't be there for them.
- They build the business largely by themselves and become the 'expert' that everyone relies on for detailed, accurate information.
- They don't care if building the business is fun, but like to think that their work might result in a significant milestone.

How a Professor Talks

"I would like to make an appointment with you to get your feedback and provide you with documentation and more information. Is next Tuesday at 2:00 pm good for you? "

Here, you will notice that Professors want to ensure that the prospect receives relevant, detailed information so they can make an informed decision, whereas the Angel will simply ask how the prospect is feeling when doing the follow up. The underlying intention below the Professor's language is, "What else do you need to know before you make a sound decision?"

The Four Sub Styles of Professors

Thinking Professor

- Focuses on possibilities
- Has a great need for privacy
- Not influenced by titles or rank
- Values precision, order and accuracy
- Avoids volatile or overly direct people

Directing Professor

- Quiet and serious
- Dependable and keeps their word
- Future focused
- Decisive

Influencing Professor

- Has a strong drive to help others
- Relates well to people but prefers a private lifestyle with few friends
- Highly aware of people's emotions
- Associates self worth with work
- Not attentive to details

Relating Professor

- Most inward acting of all styles
- Diplomatic and accommodating
- Always sees both better and worse ways to do things so can become confused by the options.
- Dislikes opposition and adversity

How to Get a Professor's Buy-In

- Prove in writing the quality and value of your product and yourself as a leader.
- Do not rush them.
- Do not embellish or over sell.
- Tell them what you think, not what you feel.
- Be prepared for them to comparison shop by emphasizing your product or opportunity's strengths.
- Give them time to study the options.
- Help them make a commitment by asking, "What else do you need to know before you make a decision?"

After the Commitment

- In your follow up information, be sure to provide education on how they can track their own progress and training.
- Ask them how they would like you to stay in touch with them, how often, and for how long.
- Discuss what the product or opportunity has accomplished and how well it has done so.
- Demonstrate cases where the product or opportunity has worked for others.
- Give them as much detailed educational material as they want. They can never know too much.

Who Do You Know?

Who do I know that is a Professor?

Who do I know that is an Angel?

Who do I know that is a Captain?

Who do I know that is an Entertainer?

Think about the people in your life: who you have easily gotten along with and who have been challenges for you. What kinds of people would you like to have in your organization who are not already there? How are you going to attract them?

Start applying the tools on the Cheat Sheet and practice communicating with different people, so you can have a more successful and fulfilling business.

The History of Quadrant Personality Typing

It all started in 370 BC with Hippocrates. He was a physician who was the first person to divide people into one of four styles that he called humors, based on which system in the body he thought predominated in a person: The Sanguine, The Phlegmatic, The Melancholic, and The Choleric.

Plato (340 BC) was interested in people's contribution to social order, so adapted Hippocrates' theory and divided people into four styles based on a social order scale. His pupil, Aristotle (325 BC) defined people based on how they seek happiness, which he called Hedonistic, Proprietary, Ethical, and Dialectical.

Almost 500 years later, the physician Galen (190 AD) developed the terms of Hippocrates and applied them to actual personality. He was the first person to promote the idea that physiology, rather than the Gods determines temperament. Another 1350 years passed before Paracelsus (1550) added his own thoughts to quadrant typology, incorporating animal names to describe Personality styles.

In the latter half of the 1800's, science began to predominate and the field of psychology changed from the study of the mind to the study of behavior, introducing the nature or nurture debate. State theory -- the belief that 'who we are' is determined solely by the environment -- emerged as a determinant of behavior for the first time. The father of behavioral psychology, Wilhelm Wundt, initiated the belief that the brain, rather than the spirit is responsible for personality, leading the way for the development of psychiatry.

The main contributor to trait theory at the time was Ivan Pavlov who, around the turn of the century, theorized that we function solely through stimulus response mechanisms – or instincts – as do other mammals, and are programmed to react, rather than respond. Freud, too, believed that we are mere animals and have no free will or self-determinism.

In the midst of this paradigm in thinking about being a human being versus being a human animal, Carl Jung appeared. He was originally a peer of Freud's but parted ways and initiated a revival in quadrant personality typing, along with the idea that we are more spirit than animal. In the 1920's he worked out a complex personality theory based on extraversion versus introversion combined with preference for one of four basic psychological functions: Thinking, Feeling, Sensation, and Intuition.

In 1958, Isabel Myers and Kathryn Briggs furthered Jung's work and developed a test based that identified sixteen basic styles, which became a favorite method for identifying career interests in universities, called the Myers Briggs Types Inventory.

After that, the Marsden DISC was developed. This was a tool used in business to identify Personality styles so human resources personnel could correctly assign people to tasks in terms of their social orientation: Driver (Red), Entertainer (Blue), Steady (Green), and Compliant (Yellow).

Chart of Quadrant Theorists and Their Types

Theorist	Type 1	Type 2	Type 3	Type 4
Hippocrates 380 BC	Blood	Yellow Bile	Black Bile	Phlegm
Plato 340 BC	Artisan	Guardian	Rational	Idealist
Aristotle 325 BC	Hedonistic	Proprietary	Dialectical	Ethical
Galen 190	Sanguine	Melancholic	Choleric	Phlegmatic
Paracelsus 1550	Salamander Impulsive	Gnome Industrious	Nymph Inspired	Sylph Calm
Marston DISC 1921	Influencer Red	Dominant Green	Compliant Yellow	Steady Blue
Myers/Briggs 1966 Based on Jung 1923	Sensation/ Perceptual (SP)	Sensation/ Judgmental (SJ)	Intuitive/ Thinking (NT)	Intuitive/ Feeling (NF)

Further Reading

Mastery: The keys to success and long-term fulfillment, by George Leonard

Now, Discover your Strengths by Marcus Buckingham and Donald O. Clifton

The Platinum Rule by Tony Allesandra
http://www.alessandra.com

Please Understand Me by David Keirsey and Marilyn Bates

Please Understand Me II by David Keirsey

Personality Plus by Florence Littauer

Personality Puzzle by Florence Littauer and Marita Littauer

Relationship Strategies by Dr. Tony Allesandra. Six CD set. This is the most useful study of the styles I have found. There are numerous examples of what people say, how they sound, how to help them in the sales process, and how to relate to them.

The Cheat Sheet

Also Available at www.CarolMerlo.com

Persuasion/Retention Cheat Sheet

Captain	Entertainer
Behaviors	
Steady eye contact	Steady eye contact
Seems impatient	'Musical' speech
Poor at small talk	Tells stories and jokes
Emphatic language	Lots of hand gestures
Firm handshake	Spontaneous touching
Persuasion	
Let them control the process	Tell them stories about people
Provide all the pertinent info the first time.	Show how we provide status, recognition and excitement
Don't give lots of details	Be enthusiastic
Use thinking words	Use feeling words
Get to the bottom line	Talk faster
Show how to gain power	No details – fun and easy
Do you want to join our business? Yes or No.	Where do we go from here?
Retention	
Send follow up information showing your commitment to their getting results.	Help with the details. Do it for them because they don't read the directions.
Ask them how you are doing with them.	Remind them they made the right choice
Provide a self-directed training system to do on their own	Show them how to use the products.
Talk business, not relationship.	Have regular contact in social situations that are fun and upbeat.

Persuasion/Retention Cheat Sheet

Angel	Professor
Behaviors	
One-on-one eye contact	Poor eye contact
Speaks slowly and calmly	Enunciates words
Good listener	Doesn't like touching
Talks about feelings	Uses analytical language
Warm handshake	Light handshake
Persuasion	
Show them you care about them	Written validation on you, product, and business
Mention names of people they know	Do not over sell
Use feeling words	Use thinking words
Focus on contribution and wholeness	Focus on details, rationale, features.
Easy and simple	Do not over sell
Provide gentle nudges to get to commitment	Make follow up calls to answer their questions
Encourage their questions so they don't regret their decision	What else do you need to know before making your decision?
Retention	
Provide consistent, hands- on training	Provide a system for tracking their progress
Provide simple communication methods	Ask them how you should support them
Show them specific steps to build the business	Focus on the results of the products and business
Maintain a friendship by having quality time with them.	Show how the product and business has worked for others

About Carol Merlo

I grew up in a suburb of Los Angeles in the sixties and started my work career as a folk singer and actor. I learned two things from those experiences: (a) I loved being able to create joy and inspiration in peoples' lives; and (b) I love the freedom that entrepreneurship affords me.

My mother was a home economics teacher who had a passion for nutrition. I learned about the importance of diet, supplements, and exercise from her. She was a tremendous role model for me.

It wasn't until 1986 when I found myself in a battered woman's shelter with my 1-year old son and few remaining possessions that I became determined to live the life of my dreams. I used loans and scholarships to put myself through school and cleaned houses to make ends meet.

I received a Master's degree in Educational Psychology after six years. I decided that what I wanted most in life to do was help people develop the self-confidence and skills to create lives of meaning and purpose,

I am dedicated to providing quality information that people can use to Create a Happy Body. I hope I have touched your life through this book.

Carol Merlo
Coppell, TX 2014

Create a Happy Body

www.CarolMerlo.com

There is a deep connection between body and mind, and it profoundly affects our physical health and well-being. In Create a Happy Body, Carol Merlo simplifies complicated information on taking care of our bodies and gives you the simple truth about how you can feel great for a lifetime.

Learn How . . .

- Deliberately choose better health habits
- Be amazed at your new ability to feel great and love the body you live in.
- Discover the powerful relationship between thoughts, emotions, and health.
- To feel GREAT each and every day.

Discover. . .

- How to use your mind to change your body.
- How to get past the Rubber Band Effect.
- The fastest way to lose body fat.
- The #1 FREE thing you can do to extend your life.
- What modern farming has done to damage your health – and what you can do about it.
- How much water you actually need to drink.
- What you really need in a dietary supplement.
- How thought impacts emotions.

Available in Soft Cover, EBook and Audio formats.

www.ingramcontent.com/pod-product-compliance
Lightning Source LLC
Chambersburg PA
CBHW060119050426
42448CB00010B/1951